MY BiG BROTHER JO JO HiS FRieND SCHiZOPHReNiA

BY: gWEN BOYD MOSS

My Big Brother Jo Jo & His Friend Schizophrenia
ISBN: 978-0-9831695-7-4
Written by: Gwendolyn Boyd-Moss
Illustrations By: Charlton "CP" Palmer

A New Day — Publishing

Published by: A New Day Publishing www.anewdaybooks.com

DEDICATION

To my sons Justin, Damon and Brandon be inspired and develop all of your gifts. You are the Best part of everything that I am!!! I Love You!!!!
-Mom

RINggggg WENT THE ALARM STARTLING US AND ALERTING US THAT IT WAS TIME TO RISE AND SHINE!!! A NEW DAY HAD BEGUN!

IN OUR HOME, EVERY DAY IS A NEW DAY,
A DIFFERENT DAY SOMETIMES FILLED WITH
TWISTS AND TURNS.

AND BIG ADVENTURES SEEN THROUGH THE
EYES OF MY BIG BROTHER JO JO AND HIS
FRIEND SCHIZOPHRENIA.

WHEN WE'RE TAKING WALKS OR PLAYING IN PARKS, JO JO SAYS "THEY ARE THERE AND THEY CAN TALK!"

I WANT TO MEET JO JO'S FRIENDS, BUT MOMMY SAYS I CAN'T.

I HEARD HER SAY THAT THEIR NOT REAL, JUST IMAGINED IN JO JO'S THINKING TANK!!

A THINKING TANK WITH FRIENDS INSIDE?
WHAT DOES THAT REALLY MEAN?
I DON'T KNOW WHAT IT MEANS, BUT I STILL
WISH WE COULD SEE!!

VISIONS OF PEOPLE AND PLACES ARE WHAT MY BROTHER SEES. SOME SEEM TO BE LOTS OF FUN AND SOME SEEM VERY MEAN.

LITTLE ELVES THAT MAKE HIM LAUGH AND BIG BAD TROLLS THAT MAKE HIM MAD.

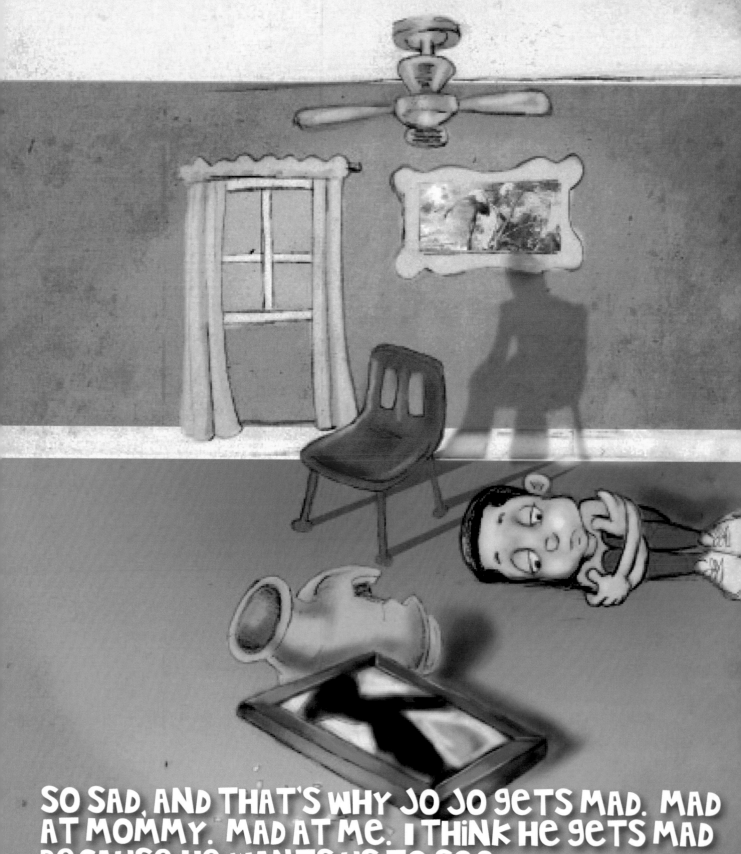

SO SAD, AND THAT'S WHY JO JO GETS MAD. MAD AT MOMMY. MAD AT ME. I THINK HE GETS MAD BECAUSE HE WANTS US TO SEE.

SEE WHO IS THERE. WHEN NO ONE IS THERE. SEE THE INVISIBLE PERSON THAT SITS NEAR HIS CHAIR.

MY BROTHER JO JO IS SPECIAL, VERY SPECIAL TO ME.

BUT HIS FRIEND SCHIZOPHRENIA IS THE FRIEND OUR DOCTOR SAYS ONLY JO JO CAN SEE.

WE KNOW THAT SCHIZOPHRENIA IS THERE, BUT TO ME IT'S NOT FAIR, BECAUSE WHAT WE SEE IT DO TO JO JO, SOMETIMES IS A FRIGHTENING SCARE!!!

BUT DOCTORS SAY THAT THIS MAY NEVER BE,
FOR JO JO IS DIFFERENT, VERY DIFFERENT
FROM YOU OR ME.

SO EVERY NIGHT BEFORE I SLEEP, I PEEK
UNDER JO JO'S SHEETS TO SEE IF
SCHIZOPHRENIA IS ASLEEP.

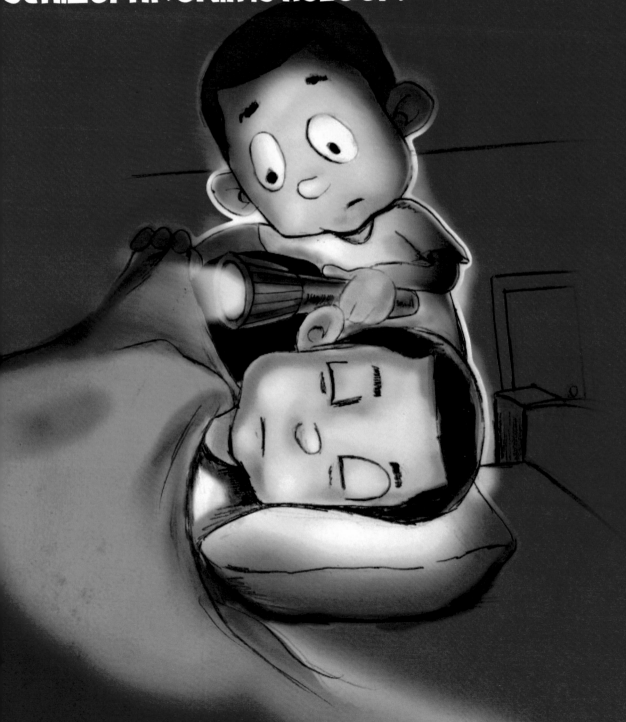

THE END.